Young Pathfinder 5

First steps to reading and writing

The Young Pathfinder series

CILT, the National Centre for Languages, seeks to promote a greater national capability in languages. CILT is a registered Charity and provides expertise and support for education, business and the wider community to help develop multilingualism and intercultural competence in all sectors of society.

CILT supports the implementation of the National Languages Strategy and has been managing the Early Language Learning Initiative on behalf of the Department for Education and Skills since 1999.

Young Pathfinder 5

A CILT series for primary language teachers

First steps to reading and writing

Christina Skarbek

First published 1998
Reprinted 2009 2004 2003 2002 2001 2000 / 10 9 8 7 6 5 4 3

Copyright © 1998 Centre for Information on Language Teaching and
Research ISBN 978-1-902031-01-9

Printed in Great Britain by Printondemand-worldwide.com Published by
CILT, the National Centre for Languages 111 Westminster Bridge Road,
London SE1 7HR. The publisher and the author acknowledge with thanks
the copyright holders who have granted permission to reproduce illustrations
from their work. It has not been possible in all cases to trace copyright
holders; the publisher would be glad to hear from any such unacknowledged
copyright holders.

Contents

Introduction

It is the aim of this Young Pathfinder to investigate just how much can be done at the early stages of foreign language teaching in the way of preparing young learners for reading and writing. While doing some useful groundwork which will hold them in good stead for their secondary school work, it is of paramount importance that the pupils should experience success and a sense of progression in these early days. Our aim should be to ensure that they remain interested and motivated enough to want to develop these skills. In many cases these children will still be struggling with the complexities of reading and writing in English. The whole process of acquiring a foreign language can be less pressured and indeed gives many children the boost they need to improve their confidence and skills in English. The aim is to get them accustomed to working with written text and for them to enjoy experimenting with words. At this age it is easier to capitalise on their natural inquisitiveness and willingness to have a go.

In order to heed the warnings of the authors of *Catching them young* (CILT, 1995):

> *Many teachers of French in particular know the pitfalls of introducing the printed form of the language too early and the dire mispronunciations that can result'* (p16)

it is important to break down the process into measured steps. This gives you a chance to reflect upon the stage at which your pupils are and to focus and adapt your activities accordingly. Throughout the book, therefore, there will be a short explanation at each step, followed by a variety of relevant activities, to help you consider why and how to proceed.

The key to the success of primary languages is doubtless the concept of continuity. Pupils must feel that the work they are doing is appropriate to their needs and they should not be presented with the same language and activities year after year, only to be met with the same scenario when they enter secondary school. In attempting to identify the stages through which we might want to guide our young learners, a conscious effort has been made in the book to avoid the use of typical secondary school resources. Considerable inspiration can be found in authentic materials, whether foreign language teaching books or real children's books of poetry and story. In much the same way as when they are learning to read and write in English, it is vital that the pupils should see a purpose in what they are doing. Their reading might help them to understand, make or do something and their writing can be valued as a record and duly displayed or targeted at a predetermined audience who will hopefully take the trouble to respond.

1. Why reading and writing

*'When should reading and writing in the foreign language
be introduced to early learners?'*
'Will it interfere with their English language work?'

Despite the fact that we all recognise the importance of children acquiring these skills, there is no doubt that their introduction seems to conjure up feelings of concern. They have come to be labelled as more difficult and less enjoyable elements of the language learning process which often seem to fill both teachers and pupils with fear and trepidation. For too long we have concentrated disproportionately on listening and speaking, to the detriment of the other two skills.

It is high time to combat these fears and misunderstandings and where better to start than with young learners who can be shown the joys of reading and writing at their own pace.

The first thing we could usefully do is to reconsider the naming of the two skills in question. 'Reading' and 'writing' carry with them a tremendous burden of expectation. They mean different things to different people. We should be thinking at this stage of 'reading' as 'decoding of symbols', acquainting the pupils with a new set of rules of interpretation and of 'writing' as 'initial experimentation with pen and paper or on a computer screen', a chance for them to play with new words.

In response, therefore, to the opening questions there is no easy answer. It is true that in most preparatory schools pupils are reading and writing French before the age of eight. The definition of 'reading' and 'writing' is very liberal, but the motivation, commitment and results are conclusive. It would seem sensible to expect young children to be receiving some initial training in these skills.

This, however, depends greatly on the individual teacher and the individual class. It is clearly essential to have discussed and agreed any such work with the teacher in charge of the class's English language work in order that your work should be seen to help rather than hinder the other. It will consist mostly in helping the pupils to match and recognise written words by recalling their visual image.

If you need to persuade colleagues, parents or your headteacher of the value of including reading and writing on the foreign language syllabus, try some of the following:

- When modern foreign languages are introduced in secondary schools, equal importance is given to Listening and Responding, Speaking, Reading and Responding, and Writing. It would seem wise to prepare pupils to work in all four skills from the start.

- Most languages are made up of a spoken and a written form and both enhance each other to make up the whole. To communicate effectively in any of these languages, both elements need to be mastered. Richard Johnstone in his superb work on *Teaching modern languages at primary school* asks us to adopt a more rounded and integrative approach to our teaching. He implores us to '*Fire on four cylinders*':

  > *Not only can reading and writing be introduced successfully, but the four modes can reinforce each other, particularly once literacy in the first language has been established.* (p65)

  He further justifies the need for young children to be adept at coping with the written word by highlighting that written communication has become almost as immediate as spoken communication through the use of fax, electronic mail and other new technology.

- Teachers have become more aware of and now appreciate that children all have their individual learning strategies. They have different strengths and weaknesses and find their enjoyment in disparate ways. Although few would argue against the desirability of hearing language before speaking it and then reading it before writing it, each child will respond at his particular level. One child has a strong visual memory and can recall vocabulary once he has seen it written down, the other has stronger aural skills and can recall the sound of new words better than their shape. The painfully shy child may prefer to sit with a book or dabble with new words while another is happier inventing and recording role plays. We need to provide all aspects of the language to all children and cannot assume that they will all be satisfied with only the spoken element.

- Pupils love it. Reading and writing can be a liberating and fascinating process, one that captivates the well-motivated learner and has been known to enthuse the de-motivated. Every teacher has experienced the child who comes up to her with a book and asks '*What does this say, Miss?*' or the desperate look of the one who wants to write on the board. This is the real world we are talking about and who are we to exclude them from it?

2. Exposing children to the written word

The first stage is purely an awareness raising exercise and involves the display of materials to which pupils will undoubtedly respond very differently. Some will notice the new additions to the classroom immediately and will refer to them frequently, others will choose to ignore them. In fact, all will take the time to look at them and that is what really matters. The key is to catch their interest and build on their knowledge in as natural and stress-free a way as possible. It is especially important to be selective about the words you choose to display and ensure that they are relevant and meaningful to the children. Their confidence can be greatly enhanced if frequent reference is made to these new cues which then come to be accepted as a useful support. Here are some examples:

 ## LABELS, POSTERS AND CHARTS

Label important parts of the classroom and frequently referred to objects such as:

> *la porte, la fenêtre, le tableau, la chaise, le stylo, le livre*
> *die Tür, das Fenster, die Tafel, der Stuhl, der Kuli, das Buch*

Some teachers even go to the trouble of labelling all the key places in the school such as:

> *la réception, la salle des professeurs, la cantine*
> *der Empfang, das Lehrerzimmer, die Kantine*

Write the date up on the board every morning, a task which you will eventually want to pass on to your pupils:

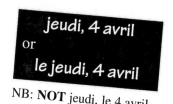

jeudi, 4 avril
or
le jeudi, 4 avril

NB: **NOT** jeudi, le 4 avril

Donnerstag, den 4. April

Attractive posters or charts can display useful areas of vocabulary, e.g. numbers, colours, days, months, etc.

Create a calender and birthday chart which can be manipulated by the pupils and might take the place of the date on the board. The French tend to lend great importance to the namesday, so it would be most appropriate to have a calender showing all the *jours de fête* and perhaps a namesday chart.

Create a weather chart which can be placed beside the English one or indeed in its place. Once pupils have become accustomed to its workings, they could be left in charge of keeping it up to date or even predicting the weather.

If your class is linked with a school abroad, this would be an ideal topic on which to begin exchanging information.

En Angleterre il fait froid. *En France il neige.*
In England ist es kalt. *In Deutschland schneit es.*

Do not shy away from using authentic foreign language posters, leaflets and brochures when they are relevant to work in other subjects. The sooner pupils realise that the foreign language they are learning in school is another means of communication and that it is only one of many which are alive and real beyond the classroom walls the better. Why not use a French train timetable when studying the 24-hour clock or a map of Spain when identifying aspects of physical geography?

 ## CLASSROOM PHRASES

Hang posters or mobiles with key classroom phrases which you will expect pupils to be using during lessons and which they invariably forget.

'Je ne comprends pas.' *'Est-ce que je peux aller aux toilettes?'*
'Ich verstehe nicht.' *'Darf ich bitte auf die Toilette gehen?'*

 ## FOREIGN LANGUAGE NOTICEBOARD

Establish a foreign language noticeboard or table on to which you will encourage your class to pin or put anything they find which has foreign writing on it. This could be confined to the language you are teaching them or indeed open to anything conveying foreign script. It is amazing to see just how many varied items can be found, ranging from postcards, letters, stamps, newspapers and magazines to labels, packets and instruction leaflets. Pupils can be inspired to display and present their findings and helped to make sense of the text through the use of semantic and phonological cues. The sort of questions you could ask include: *Where did you find this? What do you think it is for? Are there any helpful illustrations? Are there any numbers or proper names? Are there any common words?*

3. Connecting the spoken word to its written form

Once the pupils have acknowledged the presence of the written word and are beginning to comment or ask pertinent questions, they are ready to be taken a step further. This stage involves you in making a more conscious effort to link the spoken to the written form in order to encourage the youngsters to begin to do the same. They need to be shown how valuable it is for them to be able to decipher this new code so as to use it as a reference and prompt. You could, for example, make the link when practising or revising areas of vocabulary, by simply **standing beside the relevant poster,** using it as you would expect the pupils to do, by glancing at it for support or confirmation. You want them to rely gradually less on watching your lips, facial gestures and body language and more on written reference materials.

 ## USING THE TEACHER AS A SCRIBE

When revising or preparing for an activity at the production stage of a unit of work, it is often useful to brainstorm vocabulary. The teacher acting as scribe at the front of the class is showing the pupils exactly how the spoken and written forms connect. They are all watching as you actively repeat their answers and write them up at the same time. An example of this would be when you are planning a survey of, for instance, the most popular animal in the class.

'On fait un sondage, quel est l'animal préféré de cette classe?'
'Wir machen eine Umfrage, was ist das Lieblingstier dieser Klasse?'

The first thing to do would be to collect the names of all the animals in order to get the children thinking on the right lines and to help them with the construction of their questionnaires. If well done, this can save you all the bother of being asked over and over again how to write certain words. With time it will be possible to ask the pupils to take your place as scribe and show off the words they can remember to spell.

 ## SOUND BANKS

When pupils begin to ask questions about the different sounds created by the new language, it might be time to suggest the collection of new words into sound banks. You could arrange the letters of the alphabet around the room, such as is seen in many infant classrooms, and attach a piece of paper underneath onto which new words would be written or an envelope into which they could be placed. Each language will present its individual problems which may call for extra banks to be added. In French where will we put _chaise, quatre, auto_? and in German what will we do with _Schlange, eins, Auto_?

FAMILIAR GAMES

You will undoubtedly have been using games such as **pelmanism, memory, snap and dominoes** as practice activities. Until now the pupils will probably have relied upon symbols or pictures as prompts. Once the pupils are totally confident about the rules of the game and the vocabulary is well assimilated, then the pictorial cues can gradually be replaced by words. The important thing to remember is to time this so that pupils do not see the words as a threat but are rather intrigued and excited by the new challenge. It is best to introduce the changes little by little.

With cards for a **memory game** or **snap** these are the stages you would go through:

1   Retain the familiar card or piece with the addition of the appropriate word written or stuck on:

2   Replace half the cards or pieces with word only versions:

3   Introduce a new pack or set with only words:

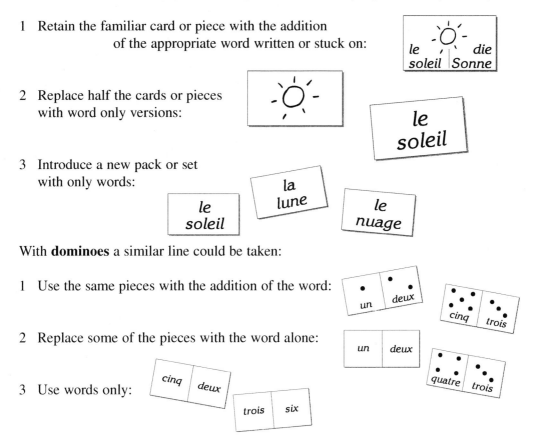

With **dominoes** a similar line could be taken:

1   Use the same pieces with the addition of the word:

2   Replace some of the pieces with the word alone:

3   Use words only:

4   Develop words into familiar sentences that could be chopped up or made up into questions and answers.

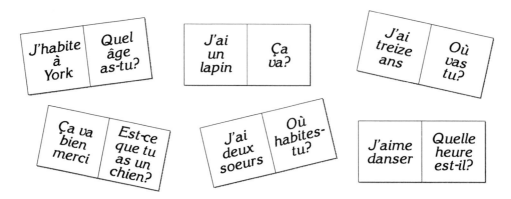

There are published games of dominoes and memory on the market and although they are authentic and attractive, they have the disadvantage of being expensive and often inappropriate for the age and needs of our pupils. It really is worth making your own materials or having them made. For some useful ideas and tips see Young Pathfinder 2, *Games and fun activities,* Chapter 7. If you have children of your own or older pupils, they will often be more than happy to help you out. They will take pride in producing attractive and appealing work and may even be persuaded to come and present them to your class.

FAMILIAR SONGS, RHYMES AND POEMS

You will also have taught your class to sing songs and recite simple poems, nonsense rhymes and *comptines.* By learning these from a good model, children can acquire accurate pronunciation and intonation patterns. In order to help them remember the texts and to add an element of variety, you will probably have used picture cues or actions. You could now replace these aids by supplying the written forms of these familiar songs and poems. The idea relies on the fact that these texts are so well-known by the pupils that they will use the words only as a reminder and will not be tempted to apply the rules of the English language to the foreign text. After sufficient exposure the suggestion is that, with their increasing confidence, they begin to read and manipulate the words to such an extent that they are beginning to assimilate the reading rules of the new language. For some children this may be a subconscious process, for others a most deliberate one. Here are some examples:

Je m'appelle Caroline, Caroline, Caroline.
Je m'appelle Caroline, Ca-ro-line.
Je m'appelle Frédérique, Frédérique, Frédérique.
Je m'appelle Frédérique, Fré-dé-rique.

(Tune 'Here we go
round the mulberrybush')

Guten Tag, Guten Tag.
Ich bin Sylvie, ich bin Sylvie.
Guten Tag, Guten Tag.
Ich bin Sylvie, wer bist du?

(Tune 'Sur le pont d'Avignon')

A good place to start is with something totally familiar and unthreatening such as introductions. If possible, names used should either be those of your pupils or of famous people whose pictures you can be pointing to. It is easy and more authentic to replace the first person form by the third. This will give good practice in the *il/elle* or *er/sie* dilemma. The French version is a fine way to introduce the notion of syllables.

Un, deux, trois, un, deux, trois.
Comment ça va? Comment ça va?
Comme ci comme ça, merci et vous?
Comme ci comme ça, merci et vous?
Ça va c'est tout.
Ça va c'est tout.

(Tune 'Three blind mice')

A chance to examine just how strange this new written system actually can be, is provided here through words and phrases that the pupils have probably been using from their very first lesson. The fact that they are now confident in the pronunciation of these words as a consequence of extensive oral practice should stop them from being thrown off course by the spelling of some of the words. Why for instance is the 'c' pronounced in different ways? The following poems can help for the same reasons. They are also based on familiar themes and have their English equivalent. The first are based around telling the time and would therefore act as useful reminders:

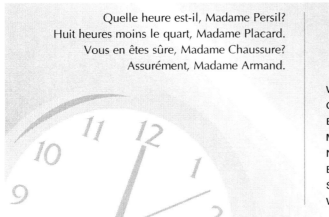

Quelle heure est-il, Madame Persil?
Huit heures moins le quart, Madame Placard.
Vous en êtes sûre, Madame Chaussure?
Assurément, Madame Armand.

Wie spät mag's sein?
Grunzt das Schwein.
Ein viertel vor sieben
Meckern die Ziegen.
Noch ein Viertel dazu
Brummt die Kuh.
Schon so spät?
Wiehert das Pferd.

The next examples are based on the well-loved finger rhyme *This little piggy went to market*, etc. The French version again throws up the problem of the '*c*' and gives the children an early taste of the perfect tense. The German version provides a novel way of reading about the members of a family.

 Ce petit cochon est allé au marché.
Ce petit cochon à la maison est resté.
Ce petit cochon a eu du rôti.
Ce petit cochon n'en a pas eu envie.
Ce petit cochon n'eut plus peta petit
Qu'à retourner chez lui.

Das ist die Mutter, lieb und gut.
Das ist der Vater, wohlgemut.
Das ist der Bruder, schlank und groß.
Das ist die Schwester, mit dem Püppchen
auf dem Schoß.
Das ist das Kindchen, zart und klein.
Das ist die ganze Familie – Patschhinein.

The lyrics of the following simple songs
also depict very basic language:

| 1 | 2 | 3 | 4 | 5 | 6 | 7 | 8 | 9 | 10 |

*U*n petit,
deux petits,
trois petits
lapins

*Q*uatre petits,
cinq petits,
six petits
lapins

*S*ept petits,
huit petits,
neuf petits
lapins

*D*ix petits
lapins sautent

Extra lyrics

poissons - nagent
oiseaux - volent
serpents - glissent
cochons - grognent
moutons - bêlent

(Tune of *Ten little indians*)

JACKPOT

Ich habe eine Banane
und die Banane ist gelb.
Sie ist oben gelb, sie ist unten gelb.
Sie ist oben unten gelb, gelb, gelb.
Ich habe eine Banane
und die Banane ist gelb.

Extra lyrics

Tomate   Karotte
Kartoffel   Bohne
Pfirsich

(Tune of *Old Macdonald*)

Easy repetitive songs like the ones opposite are ideally suited to the gradual introduction of the written form of key words. In this case the numbers have most probably already been seen so that it is only the word 'petit' that is new, alongside the *lapins* and the other animals and their movements. You could create a game in which the pupils need to link the correct label for the action or pictorial clue you give. They could be asked to point at the correct word, run to it, hold it up or place it in the correct order. Similarly with the German example, the pupils could be asked to point to or hold up the appropriate cards when singing key words.

The very same idea of linking the word that they hear with the written form could be used with the following traditional children's rhyme that exists in both French and German.

*la semaine
die Woche*

Bonjour lundi.
Comment va mardi?
Très bien mercredi.
Je viens de la part de jeudi
Dire à vendredi
Qu'il s'apprête samedi
Pour aller à la messe dimanche.

Guten Tag, Frau Montag,
Wie geht es Frau Dienstag?
Ganz gut, Frau Mittwoch.
Bitte, sagen Sie der Frau Donnerstag,
Ich käme mit der Frau Freitag
Am nächsten Samstag
Zum Kuchenessen zu der Frau Sonntag.

It is customary here to get the children to assume the roles of the days and to play out the scene as described in the poem. The days could be replaced by the names of the children.

One way of checking that they are really reading the text would be for the children to retain their roles and for you to muddle up the days in the verse. By asking them to act out the new text you are ensuring that they have read it well. Careful reading is what is required in the next verse that brings together the main prepositions.

Sur, sous, dans, devant, derrière.
devant, derrière, devant, derrière.
Sur, sous, dans, devant, derrière.
A côté de.

(Tune 'London Bridge is falling down')

This short mnemonic can be taught with actions, namely one upturned fist with the other hand demonstrating the prepositions in relation to it. An easy exercise, which would test the initial reading skills, would be to present the words individually and ask the class to reassemble the rhyme. This could either be done with small cards in envelopes for pairs to work with, or on acetate strips on the overhead projector, or with larger cards which could be attached to the board with blu-tack for the whole class to work on. It would certainly separate the *sur*s from the *sous*, both of which are difficult for British children to pronounce correctly. In addition to the problems of articulation of these new sounds, complications occur especially when there are new combinations of letters that may look similar to English eyes. The main cause of concern in German seems to be 'ie' and 'ei'.

The earlier the pupils can grasp the difference between these two the better and this little verse would be a good start.

Am Telefon

Hier ist Peter.
Wer ist dort?
Leider ist mein Papa fort.
Doch heute mittag um halb vier
Ist mein Vater wieder hier.
Bitte schön, Herr Klingelmann
Rufen Sie doch noch mal an.

This short poem practises much of the basic telephone language that can later be transferred and used in other situations. You could blank-out the names and times and get the pupils to complete their own details in order to make up their own telephone conversations.

The following poems concentrate more on specialised vocabulary rather than on constructions. They are ideally suited to gap-filling that can at this early stage rely heavily upon the recognition of the shapes of words with which the pupils have become acquainted. This recognition of word shapes is an excellent reading strategy.

Ma maison a trois étages,
Une cave et un grenier.
Au rez-de-chaussée 'y a un garage,
A l'intérieur un escalier.

Les murs sont blancs, le toit est rouge.
Les balcons sont pleins de fleurs.
Et sur la cheminée, qui bouge?
C'est mon ami, le ramoneur.

This little poem is best presented with the support of hand movements and gestures that illustrate the meaning at every stage. The pupils could eventually be presented with a gapped text either as a group exercise on the board or overhead projector or on an individual worksheet:

Ma _____a trois étages,
Une _____ et un _____.
Au rez-de-chaussée 'y a un _____,
A l'intérieur un _____.
Les _____ sont blancs, le _____ est rouge.
Les _____ sont pleins de fleurs.
Et sur la _____, qui bouge?
C'est mon ami, le ramoneur.

To begin with the pupils could be given the missing words, on separate cards or jumbled up at the bottom of the worksheet, to replace correctly. At a later stage they could be asked to write in the missing words using other reference materials or from memory. A similar activity could be done with the following German version.

In einem <u>Garten</u> wunderfein,
da steht mein <u>Häuslein</u> klitzeklein,
gebaut aus rotem <u>Ziegelstein</u>,
mit <u>Dach</u> und <u>Tür</u> und <u>Fensterlein</u>.
Das <u>Dach</u> läßt nicht den <u>Regen</u> ein,
durchs <u>Fenster</u> kommt der <u>Sonnenschein</u>,
und durch die <u>Tür</u> so winzig klein,
geh' ich hinaus, komm' ich herein.
Und will ich haben meine <u>Ruh'</u>,
schließ' ich mein <u>Türchen</u> ganz fest zu.

In einem _____ wunderfein,
da steht mein _____ klitzeklein,
gebaut aus rotem _____,
mit _____ und _____ und _____.
Das _____ läßt nicht den _____ ein,
durchs _____ kommt der _____,
und durch die _____ so winzig klein,
geh' ich hinaus, komm' ich herein.
Und will ich haben meine _____,
schließ' ich mein _____ ganz fest zu.

Similar activities would be appropriate with the next two French poems:

Je vais mettre le couvert:
<u>une nappe</u> et <u>des serviettes</u>,
puis <u>des verres</u> et <u>des assiettes</u>,
<u>des cuillers</u> et <u>des fourchettes</u>,
<u>des couteaux</u> et puis <u>des tasses</u>.
Bon appétit! Tous à vos places.

Je casse les oeufs, je mélange la pâte,
J'enlève les yeux, je pèle les patates,
Je goûte la sauce et le potage,
Je coupe le pain et le fromage,
Je brosse les souliers, je repasse,
Je lave les assiettes et les tasses,
Je fais les lits, j'essuie la poussière,
Je bats les tapis, je balaie par terre.

These examples can ideally be supported by realia at the initial stages. What better than to bring in all the necessary equipment and get the pupils to lay the table or do the house-work for you. Few will have used a tablecloth and serviettes so that this will be a good time to discuss the importance of cooking and eating in French culture. Labels could be made of all the key underlined equipment and the pupils asked to place them along-side the correct object. At a later stage the realia could be dispensed with and the labels put in the appropriate positions on the table as the rhyme is recited. For the following description in German of a snowman, realia would be less practical.

Nur aus Kugeln groß und rund.
Kohlen drin für Aug und Mund.
Oben auf den Kopf
kommt ein alter Topf.
Eine Rübe ins Gesicht
fertig ist der weiße Wicht.
Nur die Sonne fürchtet er
denn da bleibt von ihm nichts mehr.

This example does, however, lend itself to a presentation involving pictures and flashcards. One can envisage a huge outline of a snowman ready to be dressed up with his coal, saucepan and carrot. One could either replace the flashcards with word cards or produce the text without the final rhyming word of each line. In order to reconstruct the poem with the jumbled words, they would have to look carefully not only at the sound but also at the meaning of the words.

Such a reconstruction exercise would also work well with *Les chapeaux*. Here, of course, you have the additional support of the rhyming couplets. The fact that the rhyming sounds do not all look the same in the written form may well stimulate some useful discussion.

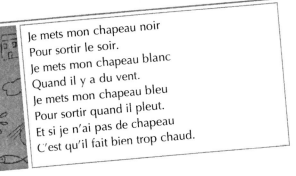

Je mets mon chapeau noir
Pour sortir le soir.
Je mets mon chapeau blanc
Quand il y a du vent.
Je mets mon chapeau bleu
Pour sortir quand il pleut.
Et si je n'ai pas de chapeau
C'est qu'il fait bien trop chaud.

STORYTELLING

You may well be telling your class familiar stories in the foreign language with the aid of picture and mime. In much the same way as with the songs and poems you could now contemplate presenting them with the written form of some key words and slowly exposing them to short, preferably repetitive texts. Children will enjoy being read to and for this the big *Sunshine books* used for teaching English are superb. The stories are interesting and the pictures attractive and helpful. You can either obtain something similar in the foreign language or attempt a simple translation that can be placed over the English script. When deciding on which books to buy or translate you should look for those which:

- encourage curiosity;
- use easily recognised and repeated patterns of language, e.g. *rhymes, repeated phrases*;
- encourage reading from left to right, both in illustrations and text;
- use clear signposts that guide the reader through a sequence of events, e.g. *soon, suddenly, on Monday*;
- use a range of techniques and devices found in books and stories, e.g. *speech bubbles, jokes, songs, references to other stories, characters*;

- encourage the reader to respond and have an opinion about what has been heard or read.

One simple way of guiding pupils from the oral to the written form of a story can be demonstrated through the example of *The House that Jack built:*

Voici la maison que Jacques a bâtie.
Voici le riz qui est dans la maison que Jacques a bâtie.
Voici le rat qui a mangé le riz qui est dans la maison que Jacques a bâtie.
Voici le chat qui a tué le rat qui a mangé le riz . . .
Voici le chien tout essoufflé qui a mordu le chat qui a tué le rat qui . . .
Voici la vache à la corne roulée qui a bousculé le chien tout essoufflé qui . . .
Voici la servante toute désolée qui trayait la vache à la corne roulée qui a . . .
Voici le fermier semant le blé qui a épousé la servante toute désolée qui trayait la vache à la corne roulée qui a bousculé le chien tout essoufflé qui a mordu le chat qui a tué le rat qui a mangé le riz qui est dans la maison que Jacques a bâtie.

The first presentation and successive practices could be organised around acetate or cardboard cutouts. The outline of the house would gradually be filled with all its contents. Once learnt and understood you could write the words on to the cut-outs and repeat the usual routine without comment. Next, the same could be done with word cards only. On the OHP it is then possible to reveal only half of the word, namely the top or bottom, e.g.

la vache   la vache

This is a far better exercise than jumbling up the letters which can create real confusion for children with reading difficulties. It is the shape of the word that is recognisable at this stage. Eventually the pupils will be reading, or more likely recognising, the key words which in turn enables them to retell the story.

There is something especially appealing about reading from a real storybook. Unfortunately, most authentic children's storybooks tend to be written in an extremely complex style which is quite unsuitable for our needs. You need to find very easy, repetitive and well-illustrated stories such as the version of *Le navet* shown on the following page. You are otherwise in the business of writing simplified versions of authentic texts or good, simple translations of the many wonderful storybooks available to you in English. When browsing through the children's books in a school library, it really does not take long to identify texts that could be used. A few such examples are: *Seven blind mice* by Ed Young, *The house that Jack built* by William Stobbs, *Ernest and Celestine* by Gabrielle Vincent, *Old MacDonald had a farm* by Holly Berry and *Bear's adventure* by Benedict Blaithwaite. These all have short, repetitive texts, clear and attractive illustrations and a simple storyline. You will find more detailed help and ideas on telling stories in Young Pathfinder 3, *Are you sitting comfortably?* (CILT, 1995).

There are also an increasing number of books on the market that introduce the occasional word in French, e.g. *Bon appétit Bertie* by Joan Knight, *Spot goes to school* and *Spot's birthday party* by Eric Hill, *Toto in Paris* by Biddy Strevens and *The tunnel* by Brian Wildsmith, which has both the French and the English version on every page.

Le Navet

Le grand-père de la petite Madeleine a planté un navet.
Le navet pousse et devient grand, très grand! Un jour,
le vieux grand-père veut arracher le navet.
Il tire, tire et tire **mais le navet tient bon!**

Le grand-père appelle la grand-mère.
La grand-mère tire le grand-père,
le grand-père tire le navet. Ils tirent, tirent
et tirent **mais le navet tient bon!**

. . .

Le petit chien appelle le petit chat. Le petit chat tire le petit chien, le petit chien tire la petite Madeleine, la petite Madeleine tire la grand-mère, la grand-mère tire le grand-père, le grand-père tire le navet.
Ils tirent, tirent et tirent **mais le navet tient bon!**

Le petit chat appelle la petite souris. La petite souris tire le petit chat, le petit chat tire le petit chien, le petit chien tire la petite Madeleine, la petite Madeleine tire la grand-mère, la grand-mère tire le grand-père, le grand-père tire le navet. Ils tirent, tirent et tirent et . . .

Oh! Voilà le navet arraché!

From *Le navet* by Annette Ziegert
(printed by Bärenreiter)

TONGUE TWISTERS

Finally, the same principle can be applied to tongue twisters which are particularly effective in training pupils in the peculiarities of a language. Having to struggle with any of the following examples entails having to read very carefully at the same time as articulating complex or new sound combinations. Here is just a taste:

Les chaussettes de l'archi-duchesse, sont-elles sèches ou archi-sèches?

Un bon chasseur sachant chasser doit savoir chasser sans son chien!

Moi, toi et le roi – nous faisons trois.

Peu à peu on peut apprendre un peu, peut-être.

En entendant on comprend et on apprend en écoutant.

Jeune Charlotte, chante encore une jolie chanson joyeuse.

Ton thé t'a-t-il ôté ta toux?

Poisson sans boisson est poison.

Schwan, weiß wie Schnee, schwimm über den See.

Schwimm, schwimm, Schwan, schwimm zu uns heran.

Schnall schön schnell die Schnallen an die Schnallenschuhe!

Knister-, Knusper-, Knäckebrot

Knackt und kracht im Mund.

Knister-, Knusper-, Knäckebrot

Ist ja so gesund.

Klitzekleine Kinder können keinen Kirschkern knacken.

Blaukraut bleibt Blaukraut und Brautkleid bleibt Brautkleid.

Zwischen zwei Zwetschgenzweigen zwitschen zwei Schwalben.

Die Katze tritt die Treppe krumm.

In Ulm und um Ulm und um Ulm herum.

4.   Enhancing initial reading skills

This step could be seen as formalising or further delving into a process that has most probably been chugging along quite happily and developing in the most suitable and enjoyable way. It would be wrong to think that these activities had to progress in a prescriptive order. The main objective should remain that of wanting the pupils to feel motivated to interpret the written form of the new language. The time comes, however, when a few rules and aids can improve motivation even further. It is at this phase more than ever that liaison with the person responsible for the teaching of reading, if it is not you, is of paramount importance. Less so because of any harm that might be done but rather to ensure good relations and thus to enhance the whole area of reading within the curriculum. You can exchange ideas and support each other in your work in a way that will inspire your pupils and ensure that they get the best possible start. Every kind of reading requires different knowledge and when faced with unfamiliar forms and content, the children will need extra special support. When considering the sort of activities that can help in this new adventure, it is worth recalling that reading is a process that involves making sense of the text through the use of semantic, syntactic and phonological cues.

Semantic: the use of life experience and textual context to work out the meaning, i.e. consider where and how it is written - what could this be saying?

Syntactic: drawing on the patterns of spoken and written language to predict possible combinations of words and phrases, i.e. consider the language patterns – are these statements or questions, positive or negative?

Phonological: checking symbol/sound associations and recognising some familiar words, i.e. which words do we already know and of which can we work out the meaning?

THE ALPHABET

One of the first things to teach them would, of course, be the alphabet. This can be done in many different ways from chanting to singing it to a well-known melody such as *Sur le pont d'Avignon* which works in both French and German. When teaching the traditional French, German, Spanish or Italian that use the Roman alphabet, you are asking pupils, with only a few exceptions, to produce a new sound to match a known form. In French you might find it helpful to present the new sounds in these seven blocks:

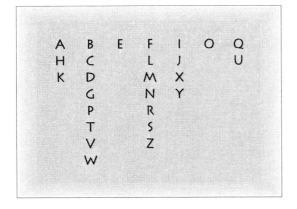

A	B	E	F	I	O	Q
H	C		L	J		U
K	D		M	X		
	G		N	Y		
	P		R			
	T		S			
	V		Z			
	W					

It is therefore imperative to fix the new sounds in the pupils' heads before showing them the letters. They will then need plenty of practice in its correct use for which you will need to find reasons to demand the spelling out of words.

- The obvious situation is that of names of people or places such as are needed when making telephone bookings. You could ask pupils to work back to back and pass firstly names and addresses and eventually entire messages to each other by spelling them out. It would be for the partner to note down the letters and decode the message.

- There is a wonderful selection of authentic materials on the market which aim to assist in the assimilation of the alphabet. In *Apprendre l'alphabet* the main character introduces us to his friends who are six families of letters. They in turn introduce us to the charm and magic of the alphabet.

- An attempt has been made to illustrate the main French and German sounds within 32 elementary words. This can be found in the Appendix on p44.

Pupils will quickly be able to identify the letters or combination thereof, which cause them the most problems when they are trying to spell words that they hear.

- The visualising of words is an exercise well worth practising. Distribute 26 large cards (A4) representing the letters of the alphabet to the class. According to the size of your class and the desired complexity of the task, you may want to include accents or additional cards of the more commonly used letters. It is then a question of choosing known words for the pupils to spell out in front of the class. The skill involves not only knowing that your letter appears in this word but also exactly in which position. The children enjoy manoeuvring themselves into the correct place and are totally unaware of the benefits of the exercise that you and the rest of the class can enjoy contemplating.

- Following on from this you could give the pupils smaller letter cards with which they would write either prescribed or their own chosen words. Once they were confident enough, a very simple version of scrabble could ensue.

- In a book entitled *Alphabestiaire* all the letters of the alphabet are represented by animals. For each animal there is a drawing and a short poem. Although the language is not easy, it is beautiful and memorable. It should be seen as a focus or starting-point and not as a test of comprehension. The verse could be read to the class and the qualities of the letter explored before the children have a go at describing and employing the letter themselves.

D *comme* dromadaire

A dos de dro de dromadaire
sous le ciel d'un blanc accablant
le désert fond d'un faux semblant
c'est son mirage hebdomadaire.

from Lander D, *Alphabestiaire* (Les Editions Ouvrières, Collection 'Enfance Heureuse')

- In German there is the *Drei Chinesen* poem which concentrates the mind superbly on the various vowel sounds. It is in fact extremely difficult to perform without the aid of the text. This is an exercise in highly disciplined reading and is at the same time very amusing both for those reading and those listening.

Dra Chanasan mat dam Kantrabaß Saßan af dar Straßa and arzahltan sach was. Da kam da Palaza: Ja was ast dann das? Dra Chanasan mat dam Kantrabaß!	Dre Chenesen met dem Kentrebeß Seßen ef der Streße end erzehlten sech wes. De kem de Peleze: Je wes est denn des? Dre Chenesen met dem Kentrebeß!
Dri Chinisin mit dim Kintribiß Sißin if dir Striße ind irzihltin sich wis. Di kim di Pilizi: Ji wis ist dinn dis? Dri Chinisin mit dim Kintribiß!	Dro Chonoson mot dom Kontroboß Soßon of dor Stroßo ond orzohlton soch wos. Do kom do Polozo: Jo wos ost donn dos? Dro Chonoson mot dom Kontroboß!

- A game of dot to dot using letters instead of numbers is a good way of making the link between the stress on letters to the words they can eventually spell. The letters, when joined together can be made to depict the meaning of the word so as to give immediate feedback.

e.g. MAISON

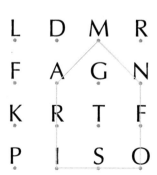

- Linking letters that have been laid out randomly in order to spell out words with their appropriate article which lead to the treasure. The skill here relies not on recognising the shape of the word but the individual letters that it is made up of.

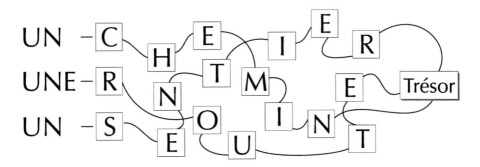

- Obliterate the same letter in all the words in a sentence for the children to identify, e.g.

    L* CHI*N JOU* DANS L* JARDIN. IL S'APP*LL* F*LIX.

    D*R HUND SPI*LT IN D*M GART*N. *R H*ISST R*X.

- Divide words into syllables and muddle them up for the children to re-order, or invest in a book or board game of *Misfits* which does the same with pictures. This is most often done with animals, e.g. KAN/GU/RUH, PAN/DA/BÄR and KRO/KO/DIL. If we take the head of one, the body of the second and the legs of the third we have a KAN/DA/DIL and a jolly good laugh. Pupils can either draw their own animals or cut them out of magazines.

- Another idea would be for them to create crazy new names for their animals by choosing from or throwing a dice for a choice of syllables, e.g.

They can choose more adventurous syllables and will then have nobody but themselves to blame when it comes to pronouncing impossible words.

	1st	2nd	3rd
1	PE	PI	PA
2	TA	TO	TU
3	SO	SU	SE
4	RU	RA	RI
5	LI	LE	LO
6	MI	MO	MU

There are other exercises we can engage the children in which will help them on their way to reading words. Simple tasks found in children's activity books such as visual discrimination, linking, matching, classifying and sequencing do not only focus on letters but are an ideal grounding in initial reading strategies. Examples of these activities are:

- identify pictures of objects that belong to the same family, e.g. clothes, fruit, vegetables, etc;
- identify pictures of objects that are associated with certain topics, e.g. winter, school, cooking, etc;
- spot the differences in two pictures or find the deliberate mistakes;
- try to spot a particular word among several others by recognising its shape.

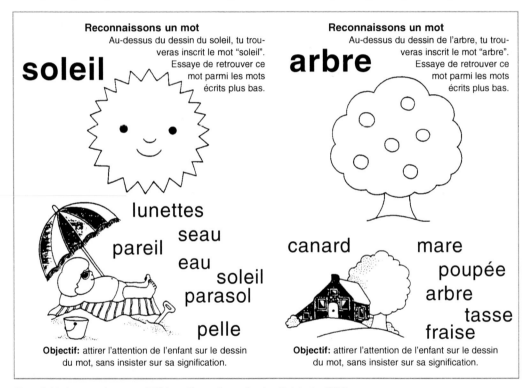

Reconnaissons un mot
Au-dessus du dessin du soleil, tu trouveras inscrit le mot "soleil". Essaye de retrouver ce mot parmi les mots écrits plus bas.

soleil

lunettes
seau
pareil
eau
soleil
parasol
pelle

Objectif: attirer l'attention de l'enfant sur le dessin du mot, sans insister sur sa signification.

Reconnaissons un mot
Au-dessus du dessin de l'arbre, tu trouveras inscrit le mot "arbre". Essaye de retrouver ce mot parmi les mots écrits plus bas.

arbre

canard
mare
poupée
arbre
tasse
fraise

Objectif: attirer l'attention de l'enfant sur le dessin du mot, sans insister sur sa signification.

From *Initiation premiers mots* (Editions Chantecler, collection Pré-école, 1985)

- match opposites e.g. small-large, inside-outside;
- identify words that begin with the same sound;
- identify the odd letter out, e.g. b b d b , s s s z , c o c c;

- colour by letter or word rather than by number. This exercise can be further enhanced when the child's instinct to colour a tomato red is being supported by the appropriate word. Perhaps the real test would be to label the tomato blue!

Rouge et jaune

Colorie la case gauche en rouge et la case droite en jaune. Regarde bien les mots écrits dans chaque case: à gauche tu vois "rouge", et à droite tu vois "jaune". Sous les dessins, les mots "rouge" et "jaune" sont inscrits. Colorie-les en suivant ces instructions.

From *Initiation premiers mots* (Editions Chantecler, collection Pré-école, 1985)

from Lauster U, *Kindergartenspiele: mein allerlustigster Zirkus* (Lentz Verlag, 1993)

During these initial stages we are relying heavily on the natural curiosity of young children to discover new things and the enjoyment they get from a variety of activities. As with all learners their motivation will be further increased if they can see the relevance of what they are learning and the progress that is being made. It would seem logical to concentrate on vocabulary that is relevant to the classroom and activities that the pupils might be required to perform. This is the method adopted by one French teaching aid *Mes 100 premiers mots à lire* and is an excellent way of preparing pupils for the use of target language rubrics that are now regulation at GCSE.

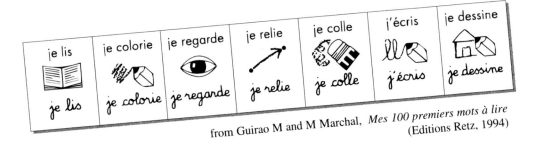

from Guirao M and M Marchal, *Mes 100 premiers mots à lire* (Editions Retz, 1994)

The accompanying symbols gradually disappear and give the pupils increasing autonomy. Autonomy is a highly desired feature of today's language learner. The same publication promotes regular review and consolidation with an opportunity to self-evaluate progress. The pupil is to colour in words he or she can read and can then colour in a petal of the flower for each of these words as a reward.

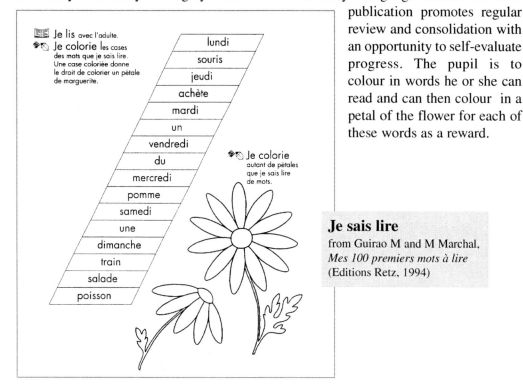

Je sais lire
from Guirao M and M Marchal,
Mes 100 premiers mots à lire
(Editions Retz, 1994)

As their confidence grows and they are recognising the shape of familiar words, they could be given strings of letters to divide up into meaningful words.

Jem'appelleSusieetj'habiteenAngleterre
IchheisseSusieundichwohneinEngland

ichheiße Susie und ich wohne hier

j'appelle Susie et j'habite ...

DICTIONARY WORK

Another area of essential groundwork is dictionary work. Much of what can be done in the foreign language is mirrored in the English language classroom and should therefore be co-ordinated. The additional feature is the bilingual nature of the dictionary, although one might choose to use monolingual ones at the start. There are some beautiful, if somewhat expensive, first dictionaries on the market. These rely on clear illustrations and are often topic based. They would certainly be an attractive supplement to your reference library and children could be encouraged to look to them for inspiration, as indeed could you. It is tempting to cut up the pictures and use them for some other activity!

Use of the bilingual dictionaries will help to develop greater pupil independence and creativity. There are several publications available on developing dictionary skills, but it is easy enough to invent your own exercises. Here are some ideas:

- Establish that there are two sections to the dictionary. Ask pupils to look up a variety of foreign and English words.

- Establish the concept of alphabetic order. Write up a selection of foreign words and see who can put them in order, e.g. *tortue, chat, lapin, souris, oiseau, poisson*
  Schildkröte, Katze, Hase, Maus, Vogel, Fisch

- Then give a list of words that all start with the same letter and see who can put them in the correct order, e.g. *mère, monsieur, mois, mai, mon, matin*
  Mutter, Mann, Monat, Mai, mein, Morgen

- Give two consecutive words from the dictionary and ask the pupils to discover which word comes next.

- Give several definitions of a word in the foreign language. Pupils must use a dictionary to establish which one is correct.

- You call out new words and the children race to be the first to stand when they are ready to read out the meaning. The race element adds to the excitement so why not use the equivalent of 'ready, steady, go!': *'prêts? 1-2-3 partez!'*, *'Auf die Plätze, fertig, los!'*

- Encourage the use of dictionaries to see associated meanings and also to help with the understanding of compound nouns: *coup de main, coup de pied, coup de soleil*
  Weißbrot, Schwarzbrot, Butterbrot

- Explain the significance of the abbreviations found after the foreign words: m, f, n and plurals. Give a list of words and ask pupils to add the gender and/or the plural form.

Once they have come to terms with the dictionary, they could be given a long word and asked to try and find as many words as they can from the one long one. *'Un mot peut en cacher d'autres'*, e.g. ELEMENTAIRE *le, la, ma, ta, rat, et, train, main, lait, matin, lire, mère . . .*

You could give them anagrams either with definitions or which would need looking up. *'Trouve l'anagramme qui existe dans le dictionnaire.'*

MIEL	>	LIME	MEIL	LIEM
ARBRE	>	RAREB	BARRE	ERRAB

You could give them a word and ask them to build from it in the following way;

MONTER
TERRE
RESTAURANT
ANTENNE

LUNE
NEUF
FIN
INDIVIDU

Pupils could be provided with or encouraged to find two-syllable words on a specific subject, e.g. eating and drinking. They must then divide the words into two by drawing a line or circle around each section, e.g. SAND/WICH FRO/MAGE CROI/SSANT BAGU/ETTE JAM/BON SA/LADE TO/MATE.

It is then for them to invent new combinations that they might like to illustrate or describe, e.g. CROIMATE.

Happy families

With the alphabet and dictionary well assimilated, the business of reading begins to take shape.

One of the first places where reading skills can be employed in an authentic but unthreatening way is in such games as *Happy families* where reading is an integral skill. One can buy a good selection of cheap card games on topics relevant to the young learner or alternatively, make your own sets of *Happy families*. Pupils will enjoy making cards of their own and then using them.

Wordsearches

Wordsearches, although too often abused, are an ideal introduction to focused reading. There are again published materials such as the series by the European Language Institute in French, German, Spanish and Italian which provides labelled words which are then found in a wordsearch on sixteen familiar and interesting topics.

LES ANIMAUX SAUVAGES EN PLACE

le crocodile

le singe

l'hippopotame

le zèbre

la girafe

le lion

le tigre

le kangourou

le serpent

from *Jeux faciles en français* (European Language Institute, 1992)

READING SCHEMES

Again concentrating on familiar and interesting vocabulary, you could construct exercises in reading comprehension with the aim of showing the pupils just how much they could already understand. One idea would be to write simple descriptions of magazine cutouts. The pictures could be hung around the classroom and the pupils encouraged to match the correct text to the appropriate picture. For a change you could provide a cartoon strip with empty balloons and a choice of phrases to place in the correct balloon. The comic strip version of *Les trois petits cochons* (Farandole2) lends itself well to such an exercise. The story is familiar, the language not too complex and the pictures are clear and supportive. You could choose initially to blank out only the key words, e.g. *loup, cochon, paille, bois, pierre* and move gradually to a total removal of all the words within the speech bubbles.

Eventually you might want to encourage regular **reading for pleasure** for which a reading scheme would be ideal. The only widely-known reading scheme created specifically for early learners is *Album des monstres* by Rosemary Bevis. It is intended to be accessible and enjoyable to all children wishing to try and read independently. The texts are minimal and take the form of very simple, meaningful and amusing dialogues. There are a growing number of reading schemes designed for secondary school, the best known of these being *Bibliobus* and *Lesekiste*. However valuable and relevant they may be, it is important to avoid using such materials unless this has been agreed with the secondary schools. The same would have to be said of the Mary Glasgow Magazines. The beginners' issues *Allons-y, Das Rad* and *¿Qué tal?* certainly have a lot to offer in encouraging reading for pleasure in a foreign language.

AUTHENTIC MATERIALS

You could make up your own reading scheme by writing your own texts or gathering together some of the plethora of authentic materials available in the form of comics, leaflets, magazines and flyers which you can so easily get hold of on a trip abroad. This would be a labour of love but a very valuable exercise nevertheless.

REAL BOOKS

Finally you could invest in some real foreign language books for your library. They would have to serve a real purpose by being actively used as inspiration or as reference materials by the youngsters as well as you. The pupils could be encouraged to look at the books and ask for clarification when necessary. After all, what we want to hear are the pupils asking to be taught to read. For you as the teacher such books may add variety and a new slant to your teaching. The sort of books referred to here are those which may well already exist in an English version and could be used to support cross-curricular work. Foreign books on art, cooking, science, geography, history, sport, to name but a few, can offer alternative aspects at the same time as highlighting the main ideas. There are also books written specifically to support parents who are helping their children to learn at home. These books are a good resource for you and help to vary your approach.

5. Encouraging initial writing skills

HANDWRITING

The first point to be made here is that this is an ideal opportunity to re-kindle and develop an interest and pride in the skill of handwriting. It is possible to make it into a novelty by teaching the basic script as it is taught to young children in the target language country. Certainly in France this is regarded as a very strict and important process. It could be pointed out to children, and indeed illustrated, that most French people's handwriting is very similar, unlike our own. You could invest in some specially lined writing paper and take the children through the exercises their counterparts in France would be expected to complete. Each letter of the alphabet in both its upper and lower case needs practising with great precision. This is an excellent exercise in hand-eye co-ordination and demands discipline and care. Many of us would agree that our children need both. It would be good to see them enjoying the art of writing through which they can experience success and a great sense of pride.

FINGER WRITING

Once they have begun to master the new script, they can practise by finger writing in the air for others to read or on the backs of other pupils. Both exercises demand concentration from both sides and help the children to visualise the letters. The same activity can then be developed using words and even phrases. There is little doubt that it will be the girls of the class who show themselves to be keener in this area, but that is no reason to stop.

A simple game of hangman (*le pendu, Galgenmännchen*) allows the pupils to practise not only spelling but also the formation of individual letters. The exercise is more valuable when performed on the classroom board for two reasons. Firstly, pupils will be more aware and therefore more careful about what and how they write in front of an audience. Secondly, it is not easy to write well on a board and will demand further concentration.

GRAFFITI

An easy way to get the pupils writing freely early on is to establish a graffiti board as suggested by Barry Jones in his Pathfinder 10, *Being creative* (CILT, 1992). A specially designated area on the wall is provided for children to write on in the foreign language.

GAMES WITH WORDS

Having enthused them to put pen to paper, they will need plenty of opportunities to stay with it. Initially, they will do little more than copy vocabulary or phrases. It is, however, worth giving them responsibility for this by encouraging them to make the work their own. Instead of copying blindly from the board or a book, encourage them to impose their own order or pattern on the work. Just as word-processing is boring until you can begin to play around with the format, size and font, so too is handwriting. They can design their own format and style of writing. A useful resource here is the series published by the European Language Institute in French, German, Spanish and Italian. It provides attractive labelled pictures of familiar and interesting topics and then muddles up the labels on the next page. The simple process of identifying the correct label before copying it out helps retention and adds challenge to the task, as indeed does filling in a crossword using the same vocabulary.

LES ANIMAUX CROISÉS

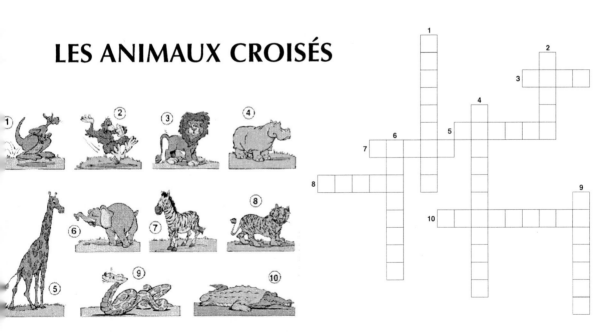

from *Jeux faciles en français* (European Language Institute, 1992)

Another good activity involves **form-filling** which can be made as complex as the pupils can cope with. Children will enjoy creating their own *Carte d'identité* or *Personalausweis* or may prefer to make one up for a personality whose picture they have cut out of a magazine.

AUTOPORTRAIT

Colle ta
photo ici

Nom: Je m'appelle . . . .

Age: j'ai . . . . . ans.

Anniversaire: c'est . . . .

Adresse: . . . .

Professeur de français: il/elle s'appelle . . . .

Ecole: . . . .

Couleur préférée: . . . .

Signe astrologique: je suis . . . .

Meilleur(e) ami(e): il/elle s'appelle . . . .

Animaux: j'ai . . . .

Famille: j'ai . . . . frères et . . . . soeurs.

Groupe préféré: . . . .

Chanteuse préférée: . . . .

Chanteur préféré: . . . .

Emission de télé préférée: . . . .

Film préféré: . . . .

Acteur/actrice préféré(e): . . . .

Plat préféré: . . . .

Boisson préférée: . . . .

POETRY

Having stressed the value of handwriting for its own sake, now let us turn to the personal and creative outcomes that this skill opens up to us.

Poetry or imaginative composition has long been recognised as one of the best ways to encourage individual writing. The aim is to stimulate children to create through the written word. This can start in a very simple way with what is known as concrete or shape poetry. The idea rests on linking the image of a word with its written form, but rather than labelling a picture the two are incorporated into one in a personal and creative way. It may be that the word can be decorated appropriately or the picture marked.

Gradually there is a move away from the supporting symbol or illustration and the child feels able to express himself with words alone. The first attempts may take the form of acrostic poetry. A familiar and meaningful word is chosen that should evoke some sort of thought in the children. The task is then to build words around the letters of this core word. This might result in a random list of words but could equally lead to the production of something eloquent.

Bonjour
Olivier
Nathalie
Jacqueline
Odette
Jacq**U**es
Au **R**evoir

USING A STRUCTURE OR FRAMEWORK

The very limited vocabulary of these young learners is likely to restrict their creativity unless they are given a simple structure or framework around which to construct their poems. At first the pupils can be asked to change only a few details before eventually being encouraged to develop their own ideas on the same lines. The poem entitled *L'ogre* is effectively no more than a list of the food that this monster consumes in a day. It becomes increasingly more ridiculous, but therein lies its potential appeal.

J'ai mangé un oeuf, deux langues de boeuf,
Trois rôts de mouton, quatre gros jambons,
Cinq rognons de veau, six couples d'oiseaux,
Sept immenses tartes, huit filets de carpe,
Neuf kilos de pain, et j'ai encore faim!
Peut-être ce soir, vais-je encore devoir
Manger mes deux mains
Pour avoir enfin, le ventre bien plein.

Children will initially be disgusted by the notion of eating such things as kidneys and tongues, not to mention the final move to cannibalism.

Sensitivity will certainly need to be shown towards vegetarians until they have understood that they can now replace all the items of food for those of their own choosing. How about inventing a menu for a vegetarian or one consisting entirely of their favourite foods.

Another easy way of setting them off is by providing them with **rhyming verse** that can be added to. It is important to stress the fact that creativity takes precedence over meaning in the initial stages. We want children to enjoy manipulating new words that they have identified as rhyming.

A Paris, à Paris
Sur un petit cheval gris
A Nevers, à Nevers
Sur un petit cheval . . .
A Issoire, à Issoire
Sur un . . .
A Rouen . . .

Wer mag die Tomate – Agathe, Agathe.
Ist rot und so rund, ist gut und gesund.
Wer mag Petersilie – Odilie, Odilie.
So schneide sie fein, in Süppchen hinein.
Wer mag die Karotte – Charlotte, Charlotte.
So zieh sie heraus und trag sie ins Haus.

Food and forenames in German and towns and colours in French will keep our young learners occupied for a while in a quest to be as original as possible. This next German verse has both a structure and a rhyme which could be adapted. Pupils could either think of objects they know which rhyme with other colours, e.g. *rot/Boot, weiß/Reis,* or ignore the rhyming and find new objects to paint.

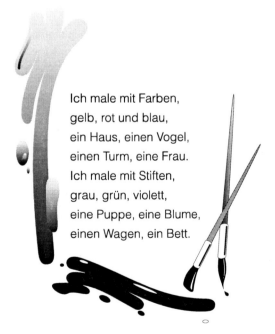

Ich male mit Farben,
gelb, rot und blau,
ein Haus, einen Vogel,
einen Turm, eine Frau.
Ich male mit Stiften,
grau, grün, violett,
eine Puppe, eine Blume,
einen Wagen, ein Bett.

The next step might be to provide verses that are based around **one linguistic feature**. Once confident in the particular structure, the pupils can begin to build their own new meanings and be more adventurous in their use of new vocabulary.

This little French verse immediately asks pupils to make additions once they have grasped the central structure of *j'ai...* *...pour + infinitive.*

Et j'ai un nez pour sentir.
J'ai une bouche pour rire
Pour manger et pour parler.

Et j'ai aussi sur les côtés
Deux oreilles pour écouter.

Qu'est-ce que tu as encore?

J'ai deux mains pour écrire
Pour peindre, pour applaudir.

J'ai deux pieds pour marcher
Pour courir et pour sauter.

Heute ist ein Tag, an dem ich <u>singen</u> kann.
Heute ist ein Tag, an dem ich <u>singen</u> kann.
Ist das nicht ein Tag, an dem ich froh sein kann?
Ja, das ist ein Tag, an dem ich froh sein kann.

2   lachen
3   klatschen
4   rennen
5   schnarchen
6   flöten

The main structure practised in this German song does not seem too difficult in this particular context, and yet it is quite demanding. All the more reason to assimilate it sub-consciously.

Here only the verb is being replaced and many more examples could be added. If you wanted to develop this further, other elements could be changed. *Tag* could become *Monat* or *Jahr* so that *heute* could become any day or month and *kann* could become any one of the other modal verbs.

There are further poems that provide creative frameworks in that they offer an outline and allow us to be inspired to make this our own.

A Paris il y a une rue
Dans la rue il y a une maison
Dans la maison il y a une chambre
Dans la chambre il y a une table
Sur la table il y a un vase
Dans le vase il y a des fleurs.

Fleurs dans le vase
Vase sur la table
Table dans la chambre
Chambre dans la maison
Maison dans la rue
Rue à Paris

The way to present this poem is again by using accompanying actions that in turn aid memorisation. Once the pupils have visualised the effect of zooming in and out of the poem, they could be made to think about replacing Paris for another town and perhaps finding an alternative for the flowers on the table. The more confident could think about putting the focus on their school or home. *A cette école il y a une classe. Dans la classe il y a un tableau. Sur le tableau il y a . . .* On the opposite page you will find another version of the same poem that might be more appropriate as a writing exercise when the pupils will be expected to recall and write out the vocabulary represented by the symbols. In German a similar poem exists:

Mein Vater kaufte sich ein Haus.
An dem Haus war ein Garten.
In dem Garten war ein Baum.
In dem Baum war ein Nest.
In dem Nest war ein Ei.
In dem Ei war ein Dotter.
In dem Dotter war eine Laus.
Eins, zwei, drei und du bist raus!

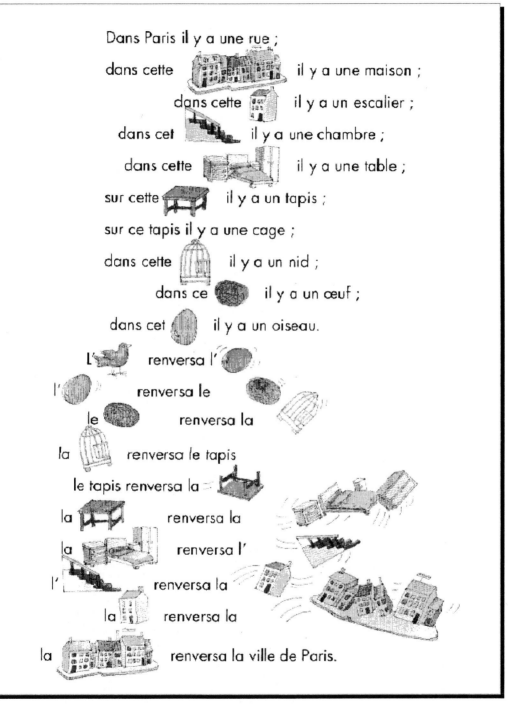

Dans Paris il y a une rue ;

dans cette il y a une maison ;

dans cette il y a un escalier ;

dans cet il y a une chambre ;

dans cette il y a une table ;

sur cette il y a un tapis ;

sur ce tapis il y a une cage ;

dans cette il y a un nid ;

dans ce il y a un œuf ;

dans cet il y a un oiseau.

L' renversa l'

l' renversa le

le renversa la

la renversa le tapis

le tapis renversa la

la renversa la

la renversa l'

l' renversa la

la renversa la

la renversa la ville de Paris.

Eluard P, excerpt from *Invraisemblance et hyperbole* in
Le Hellaye C and D Barzotti, *Farandole 2* (Les Editions Didier, 1993)

By adapting the first line, you could use the same zoom effect on this poem, e.g. *Mein Bruder kaufte sich ein Auto. In dem Auto war ein . . .* It also helps the pupils to think about different and perhaps less familiar topics. The next German verse, entitled *Das Rezept,* offers us the chance to replace the weather vocabulary by food and thus create a real recipe. This works well with a *Fruchtsalat.*

Man nimmt ein bißchen Sonnenschein.
Vermischt ihn gut mit Regen.
Rührt Wind und Wolken mit hinein.
Und Schmutz von allen Wegen.
Gibt Schnee dazu, soviel man will.
Und fertig ist er, der April.

 OPPOSITES

An alternative to providing a framework and allowing children to adapt details within a sound structure is to get them thinking about opposites or contrasts. Yet again they can thus concentrate their energies on the words they want to use and not have to worry too much about making syntactic mistakes. This makes them feel secure and often gives them the courage to be more inventive. Barry Jones exemplifies this idea beautifully in his Pathfinder 10, *Being creative*, where the first four lines of a poem are given and the pupils asked to continue it starting each line with either *Bonjour* or *Au revoir.*

Bonjour matin,
Au revoir sommeil.
Bonjour devoirs,
Au revoir liberté.

The same could be done with *Ici* and *là-bas* or *Avant* and *maintenant* and has already been done with likes and dislikes. A chance to read someone else's and to formulate one's own thoughts without having to justify them is a chance not to be missed. The beauty of such an exercise is that all the pupils can produce a piece of written work that looks good, reads well and makes sense to them.

J'aime la télé
J'aime les BD
J'aime mes copains
J'aime les bouquins
J'aime mes parents
Pépés et mémés
Mon chat et le vent
Lucky Luke, les fées.

Mais je déteste
Oh je déteste
Quoi?
Devinez . . .
Je déteste avoir du sable
Entre les doigts de pied
En rentrant de la plage
L'été . . .

This poem exemplifies perfectly just how private and simple a poem can be. The same idea of using opposites lends itself well to adjectives. How about comparing large with small things, old with new or good with bad?

In this example the framework does no more than set one word against its opposite. Having established the pattern and attempted to add to the list of adjectives, you could pick up on the final two lines and suggest that the pupils make less obvious comparisons that are personal and evocative, such as exemplified in this French verse:

Alt ist	nicht neu
Neu ist	nicht alt
Warm ist	nicht kalt
Kalt ist	nicht warm
Reich ist	nicht arm
Arm ist	nicht reich
Groß ist	nicht klein
Grob ist	nicht fein
Dunkel ist	nicht hell
Langsam ist	nicht schnell
Eckig ist	nicht rund
Schwarz ist	nicht bunt
Schmal ist	nicht breit
Eng ist	nicht weit
Sauer ist	nicht süß
Händ sind	keine Füss
Füss sind	keine Händ
Das Lied hat	kein End

Noir	n'est pas	blanc
Petit	n'est pas	grand
Vert	n'est pas	gris
Là-bas	n'est pas	ici
Ici	n'est pas	là-bas
Maman	n'est pas	Papa

This short verse with its poignant ending highlights the fact that very straightforward phrases can develop into highly complex thinking. It is often the writer alone who understands exactly what he or she is wanting to say, but it is the process and satisfaction with the result that concern us most at this point.

There are then the many other poems that act as stimuli to the individual reader because of the picture that they paint or the appeal of the subject matter. This little verse about a rabbit certainly appeals to young animal lovers and can be used as a spring board when they want to write about their own beloved pets.

Il est petit et rond et blanc et doux.
Il mange des herbes, du pain, du sucre, des choux.
Il a des yeux tout rouges. Des griffes, une queue.
Il a de grandes oreilles, mon lapin russe.

A final suggestion for presenting a framework without a poem consists in supplying the pupils with a pattern around which to work. They could for instance be answering a series of questions:

Qui? Quoi? Où? Quand? and *Pourquoi?*   *Wer? Was? Wo? Wann?* and *Warum?*

Alternatively they could identify perhaps four features with which they will go on to describe famous people, e.g. Nationality/ Hobby/ Place/ Clothing – Michael Jackson

Il est américain. Il aime jouer avec son singe, Bubbles. Il va au zoo. Il porte un short et un T-shirt.
Er ist Amerikaner. Er spielt gern mit seinem Affen, Bubbles. Er geht in den Zoo. Er trägt eine kurze Hose und ein T-Shirt.

PERSONAL AND CREATIVE WRITING

The ultimate step would then be to encourage the pupils to create their own written work in whatever format and on whatever subject inspires them. They may want to begin with slogans, adverts, cartoon strips or posters for display before launching themselves into producing longer texts. Here are some ideas:

* Captions for speech bubbles either blanked out or stuck on to magazine cutouts of people in various situations.
* Create a menu for a specific person, e.g. vegetarian, baby, dog . . .
* Write the instructions for a treasure trail.
* Write new lyrics to a known melody or a rap.
* Write the script for a video production that you may eventually send to your partner school.
* Write the script for a fashion show.
* Write a diary; this could be a personal or class diary.
* Write a simple letter to a partner school.
* Create a party invitation with all the information needed plus more.
* Write a shopping list for a dream picnic or holiday.
* Make up a crossword and design your own clues.
* Create 'Wanted' posters using magazine pictures or real photographs.
* Write letters to famous people, you may even get an answer!
* Create your own recipes, e.g. a witch's brew, a magic soup or a monster sandwich
* Write your own little story books.
* Create your own recipe books of favourite or made-up recipes.
* Advertise your school, town, sports club.
* Write a Christmas or birthday present list for yourself or a famous personality.

Use of IT

Good classroom practice uses IT to enable and enrich effective language learning. It is seen as a means to an end and not as an end in itself. At its most basic, it allows high-quality written work to be achievable by all, even those with learning difficulties. Correction of errors is non-threatening and re-drafting is painless and fast. It gives the children time to think about the essence of the work they are presenting to you for correction rather than the mechanics of it. It also helps you avoid the dilemma of having to display work with major mistakes in it. There can be a considerable amount of valuable reading practice involved in performing many of the tasks. More importantly perhaps, the computer allows you to present and provide practise in many of the ideas mentioned above in a new context. It gives the pupils scope for copying, manipulating and creating.

- Such things as classroom language, paradigms, vocabulary, songs and poems can be copied, personalised and printed by the pupils for display on the classroom walls. Booklets and newsletters can be produced for visitors home and abroad.

- The simplest and potentially most boring exercises such as vocabulary learning, comprehension questions and grammar exercises can seem more glamorous when programmed on to a computer screen.

- A simple word processor will let you perform most of the various exercises outlined in previous chapters. Features such as underlining, highlighting, moving and deleting will add to the variety of presentation and practice. Missing letters and words can be filled in, jumbled letters and words can be used to make up words and phrases, continuous text can be broken up into meaningful chunks, genders and plurals can be inserted where necessary and foreign words can be matched with their English meanings or synonyms.

- All the examples given of poems and songs that provide a framework for writing can be used equally well on the screen. In addition, it is possible to type in the model of a text such as a letter and ask the pupils to change certain details.

- Finally, because correction is so easy, pupils can be encouraged to use fantasy and imagination in practising creative writing. Most of the suggestions made previously could be adopted here.

If your school can afford it, there is some good text manipulation software on the market. Do go and try it out before spending too much money and perhaps finding that it does not suit your needs. It is also worth checking that it is not already in the possession of another member of staff. Here are some examples:

- *Fun with Texts* (Camsoft) allows the teacher to type in any piece of text that can then be manipulated, developed or predicted through the use of seven different activities. These include gap filling, line reordering and decoding.

- *Tray,* of which there are many versions, is another text reconstruction package.

- *Gapkit* (Camsoft) is a versatile authoring package for gapped texts.

- *Matchmaster* (Wida Software) is a multiple-activity pair-matching program.

- *Wordsquare* will create wordsearches for you at different levels after the required vocabulary has been typed in.

There is also a place for non-text based software in language learning. Graphics packages can be used to enhance posters, pamphlets and other display work. They can also provide symbols and images that can be moved around in order to show understanding.

There is a selection of subject-specific software that also needs scrutinising before you decide to buy, but beware of poaching materials that might be used in secondary schools. Here are some of the more popular programs:

- *Quelle tête* (CUP) enables pupils to build up a picture of a face. It requires the pupils to read in order to make their choice of, for instance, short, curly as opposed to long, straight hair. As soon as they have made their choice, the feature is added to the outline of the face, thus providing immediate feedback.

- *Jeu des ménages* (CUP): the same principle as above applies to moving furniture within a house.

- *Granville* (CUP) simulation of a holiday in a French seaside town.

- *Centre-ville* (AVP) practises directions, colours and telling the time.

- *Six French games* (AVP) covers topics such as: days, months, weather, school subjects, finding the way, leisure activities, fruit and eating out.

- *Six German games* (AVP) as for the French version.

The ultimate that this maze of technology can offer our pupils as far as reading and writing are concerned must surely be electronic mail. A chance to communicate spontaneously through the medium of written text has got to be the best motivation we can provide our pupils. Many schools are already involved in fax links that afford a wonderful opportunity for our youngsters to exchange thoughts, facts and creative work.

If you want to find out more about learning languages with technology, consult NCET and the CILT InfoTech series for ideas and advice.

Appendix

LA PRONONCIATION FRANÇAISE

asseyez-vous	ligne
baguette	maison
bonjour	neuf
château	orange
couleur	porte
deux	quatre
élève	regardez
famille	six
feuille	trois
garçon	un
gentil	une
huit	vélo
ici	wagon
jaune	xylophone
kilo	yeux
le	zéro

DIE DEUTSCHE AUSSPRACHE

Apfel	Pfennig
Banane	Problem
Computer	Quark
Deutsch	rechts
Elefant	singen
fünf	Schule
Fußball	Stuttgart
Gras	spielen
Haus	Tennis
ich	und
ja	vier
Käse	wir
links	Xylophon
Mai	Yoga
nein	zwölf
Oktober	zwanzig

Useful sources and resources

USEFUL SOURCES

Berwick G and P Horsfall, *Making effective use of the dictionary* (CILT, 1996)
Guide pratique — Français Langue Etrangère (CEFISEM de Strasbourg, 1992)
Hewer S, *Text manipulation: computer-based activities to improve knowledge and use of the target language* (CILT, 1997)
Johnstone R, *Teaching modern languages at primary school* (SCRE, 1994)
Jones B, *Being creative*, (CILT, 1992)
Kavanagh B and L Upton, *Creative use of texts* (CILT, 1994)
Martin C, *Games and fun activities* (CILT, 1995)
Martin C, *Let's join in! Finger and action rhymes* (CILT, 1998)
NCET, *Modern Languages Information Files*
Satchwell P and J de Silva, *Catching them young* (CILT, 1995)
Satchwell P, *Keep talking. Teaching in the target language* (CILT, 1997)
Swarbrick A, *Reading for pleasure in a foreign language* (CILT, 1990)
Tierney D and P Dobson, *Are you sitting comfortably? Telling stories to young language learners* (CILT, 1995)

RESOURCES

Bevis R, *Album des monstres* (Language Centre Publications, 1995)
Charnet C, *Mon livret d'écriture et de lecture* (Hachette, 1993)
Guirao M and M Marchal, *Mes 100 premiers mots à lire* (RETZ, 1994)
Le Hellaye C and D Barzotti, *Farandole* 1 and 2 (Didier/Hatier, 1992)
Initiation premiers mots (Chantecler, collectio pré-école, 1985)
Jeux faciles en français (European Language Institute, 1994) — also available in German, Spanish and Italian
Lander D, *Alphabestiaire* (Les Editions Ouvrières, Collection 'Enfance Heureuse', 1980)
Lüber R und Mitarbeiter, *Praxishilfen für den Kindergarten* (Herder Freiburg im Breisgau, 1991)
Meyer-dreux S, *Trampoline* (CLE international, 1994)
Milou C, *Apprendre l'alphabet* (Sermap-Hatier, 1983)
Paccagnino C and M Poletti, *Kangourou* 1 and 2 (Hachette, 1991)

USEFUL ADDRESSES

National Council for Educational Technology, Science Park, Coventry CV4 7EZ.
Tel: 01203 416 994